in

An anthology of love, longing and loneliness

Volume V

Mistakes were made in life, love, spelling and grammar.

Disclaimer:

Due to a filing error on our part the physical copy paper
stock is different. Volume I - VII are on glossy stock and
Volumes VII - XII plain stock. If you are unsatisfied,
please reach out at the above email address.

Thank you

Just give me
A shoulder
To cry on
Don't judge
Just love
Allow me
To be vulnerable
Naked
A man
As I fall apart
In your hands

I'm sorry
That she's
In the way
That she's
Created this barricade
This heart-shaped vault
With nothing more
To treasure then her IOU

"Love"
She gets it
From all angles
But none
Worthy enough
To fulfill her heart

I fall for her infidelities
Due to the spell she weaves
I sit there, I beg and plead
Telling her
I'll be her love slave
As long as she never leaves

Apparently
She was only good enough
To be stood up
She sits at a table for two

I love you
I say that now
Because
It's the kindest gesture
I can think of

Inevitably
You and I
Will fade into memory
And
This is the best
I have at the moment

Let me tell you
How I'm always surprised by hugs
How I'm just so shocked
By the love
That someone's giving me
Human contact
That someone's holding me
Embracing me
And I
Don't know how to respond back
Cuz
I don't know how

Because
I am so isolated
I'm in awe
That someone treats me
Like a human being
And I just don't know how
To shake off the ice
As I melt in your arms

She's tarnished
By his name
Branded
On her halo
A slave
To his reputation

Love
Is such a powerful force
In the wrong hands
It can be
Devastating
But
In the right ones . . .

Heartbroken
Not due to the fact
She didn't love me
Nor I her
It's that no matter how hard
We tried it just didn't work out

I'm not asking
For your heart nor a smile
Only in a joke
I'm just putting forth effort
To make you happy
Whatever it takes

I want my lips
To be in sync
With yours
Like when you sing along
With your favorite song

I hate to break a heart
But sometimes
I do
You just wait
Till I find a wife
To which
I say
I do
Then how many hearts
Will I have broken

Takes
Eight
Letters
To
Say
I
Love
You

Taken
By
A
Touch
Though
A
Glace
Enough

With
Every
Intention
Of
Intimacy
She
Felt
Incompatible

Touch
Me
All
Within
And
All
Without
Feeling

My
Lips
Scream
For
The
Caress
Of
Hers

She's
Golden
Without
Ever
Being
Touched
By
Midas

She's
The
Touch
Of
Honey
In
My
Tea

I like you
Right where you are
At a distance
So my imagination
Can run away
With fantasies
How to love you
Without hurting either of us

What if
Beauty was defined
By your evilest deed
Then how pretty would you be

Skipping beats
Like skipping stones
Across a lake
I give to you
My heart to take

My hearts torn
Trapped within
Loves labyrinth

I have the words
But I haven't the heart

She was the Sunrise
I wish to set
The one
I'd much rather forget
Nothing more
Nothing less
Erased
From my thoughts
If her name were to come up
I would draw a blank
As if it weren't etched into my heart
I'd rather the darkness
Than the flickering light of her smile
The echoing joy of her laugh
The painful memory of our happiness
Now nothing more
Than a hunting past

I hold no grudge
Against the rose
Who'd pricked me
With her thorn
I should have admired
From a distance
Rather than
Threaten her existence

I've been on the cusp
Of love and lust
The eclipse of her lips
Between the light and dark
The love of a hateful heart

Your love
Is but a farce
A lie of the hollows
Where most
Would have a heart
Your emotions run shallow

I've entertained infidelity
I wear the shame
Of the spell she weaves
I grieve
I weep
I hurt
When she leaves
This masquerade
Has mastered me
And I
The slave
Of make believe
The lashes of your loveless lips
Have scarred my heart
And do not forgive
Nor forget
And I'm reminded
With every beat
How my love
Has gone undeserved
I cherish your lies
As if someday they'll become truth
But for now
Take your leave
And I'll wait here patiently

I lay naked
And listen
To the sounds
Of my body
As they scream
For your touch

Made in the USA
Middletown, DE
12 October 2022

11731907R00020